To Mr. and Mrs. D. Paul Huffman
With the Love and Compliments
of Father and Mother.
Feb. 2, 1937

JOB A WORLD EXAMPLE

Job a World Example

(*Revised Edition*)

By
JASPER ABRAHAM HUFFMAN, D. D.

Author of "Redemption Completed," "The Progressive Unfolding
of the Messianic Hope," "Voices from Rocks and Dust
Heaps of Bible Lands," "Youth and the
Christ Way," "Building the Home
Christian," "A Guide to the
Study of the Old and
New Testaments,"
etc., etc.

PUBLISHED BY
THE STANDARD PRESS
MARION, INDIANA

Copyrighted by
The Bethel Pub. Co.

Dedicatory

TO OUR SONS, D. PAUL, S. LAMBERT
AND JOHN ABRAM,
WHOM GOD HAS GIVEN US, AND WHOM
WE HAVE GIVEN BACK
TO HIM
IN SINCEREST CONSECRATION,
THIS LITTLE VOLUME
IS AFFECTIONATELY DEDICATED.

FOREWORD

THE author of this volume had been conducting Bible Conference work in various summer camps, which were attended by a large number of ministers, as well as many laymen. The Book of Job had been studied in a number of camps with increasing interest.

Occasionally requests were made for the studies in printed form, but little attention was given to the suggestion. It was at the Miama Valley, Ohio, camp that the demand for the lectures became so insistent that the responsibility could no longer be avoided.

During the ten days the Bible study hour had been cumulatively interesting. Ministers and others confessed themselves thrilled by the truth brought from this neglected book of the Bible. At the close of the last day, Rev. Bud Robinson, an evangelist of wide experience, who had been one of the engaged workers of the camp, and who had assumed the role of a disciple in the Bible Study hour, arose and called upon the class to join him in pledging the author to prepare the studies in book form. The demand was so unanimous and insistent that it could not be turned aside, and this volume is the fulfilment of the promise made that day. The demand for such a book evidences the hunger of Christians for Biblical instruction.

The Book of Job is little understood; in fact, much misunderstood. A lack of correct perspective upon the book as a whole has led to a variety of interpretations. There is danger of getting lost in the poetic part, unless one gets proper direction in the prose prologue at the beginning, and confirms his position in the prose epilogue at the close. The interpretation to the book must be found mainly in its prose parts.

There are a number of incidental teachings in the book which have been promoted to major places in the various schemes of interpretation, even by interpreters of no mean reputation. "The Philosophy of Human Suffering," "Divine Justice," "The Human Quest for a Divine Mediator," are subjects which are prominent in the book, but they are incidental and minor, contributing to the real purpose of the book. One good Calvinistic writer observes, "that the final perseverance of the saints is beautifully illustrated" in the book.

Presumptuous as it may appear, the author sincerely believes that he has discovered the proper interpretation of the book, which is, in part, indicated by the title, and which is more fully disclosed throughout the volume.

It is to be regretted that the minds of many good people are prejudiced against the man Job, and sincere ministers speak of Job as a "self-righteous man being justly punished." Of course Satan is pleased to have men ally themselves against Job, for he has failed to indict him, and in this attitude of men Satan must find some comfort.

It would appear that all good people should be found upon God's side in the evaluation of Job, even though they find themselves unable to answer all the questions which arise. There can be no question but that God was on Job's side.

The American Standard Version is quoted throughout the book, because the writer considers this the most accurate English translation of the Old and New Testaments.

May the author humbly ask that his readers peruse the volume in the spirit in which it was written, and, if any false or unwarranted conclusions are found, to report them to him, who will receive such information thankfully. If the book proves a blessing to you, dear reader, will you not speed it on in its mission of love and helpfulness? Sincerely,

J. A. HUFFMAN.

Marion, Indiana.

NOTE CONCERNING REVISED EDITION

THE first edition of this book, which was an exceptionally large one, was exhausted in a surprisingly short period of time. It was appreciated in America, where it was read by thousands. It was also adopted for use in schools where courses in Old Testament were given.

But its ministry was not confined to the homeland. In far-off China, missionaries found it so well adapted to meet a need for the training of native workers that they translated it into the Chinese tongue. It has also been greatly used in other lands.

Now that a new edition is to be published, the author wishes to take the opportunity to thank the Christian reading public for the reception which it gave to this volume when it first appeared. The persistent demand for the book compels the new edition.

There is comparatively little change which the author considered necessary. He has used the volume as a text in Bible classes in his College and Divinity School work, thus submitting it to the anvil of the classroom, urging his students to give critical consideration to his treatment and conclusions. This test the book has stood unchallenged.

The book has been revised slightly here and there, for the sake of improvement. The largest contribution to the treatment will be found in connection with Job's Lamentation of chapter three, where an important and interesting discussion will be found. The careful and critical answer to the question, did Job curse God, as Satan said he would adds a distinct value to this edition.

TABLE OF CONTENTS

Chapter		Page
I.	Introduction to the Book	15
II.	A Perfect Man	23
III.	The First Challenge	31
IV.	The First Trial	37
V.	The Second Challenge	45
VI.	The Second Trial	51
VII.	The Third Trial	59
VIII.	Liberal and Conservative Views	69
IX.	The First Cycle of Speeches	75
X.	The Second Cycle of Speeches	89
XI.	The Third Cycle of Speeches	99
XII.	Divine Intervention	107
XIII.	Job Vindicated and Rewarded	115

CHAPTER I

INTRODUCTION TO THE BOOK

CHAPTER I

INTRODUCTION TO THE BOOK

THE first thing necessary to accomplish, in our approaching the study of the Book of Job, is to brush aside indifference and irreverence. So long has the Book of Job been looked upon as practically a useless book, except to find an isolated quotation or text here and there, that but few know what the book contains. Others have felt at liberty to treat its principal character, Job, with a large measure of irreverence and to compare their troubles and trials to those of this Bible character, requiring the "patience of Job."

Then, too, the battle-ground of orthodox teachers against higher critics and liberal interpreters has been partly, for the last few years, the Book of Job. This fact makes the treatment of the book more difficult but, at the same time, more interesting.

In the order in which the sixty-six sacred books constituting the Bible are placed the Book of Job is the eighteenth. It is classed with the poetic books, since a large part of it was written in the form of Hebrew poetry.

Authorship

The fact that the book carries the name of Job is not sufficient evidence that the book was written by him, although that fact would not militate against his authorship. What we are to understand is, that the book is written of, or concerning Job, rather than by him.

The authorship remains unsettled, although the book has been ascribed to a large number of persons ranging from Moses to Hezekiah. Among the persons named by various scholars, whose writings the book may be, are Elihu, Solomon, Isaiah, Hezekiah, Baruch and Moses. Tradition claims that Moses wrote the Book of Job. The Talmud, which is a sort of Jewish commentary of the Old Testament Scriptures, also testifies to Mosaic authorship of the book.

Age or Antiquity of the Book

The date of the writing of the Book of Job is also unsettled. If we knew positively who wrote the book, we could determine more accurately when it was written; but, the authorship being uncertain, we are obliged to look elsewhere for this information.

Higher criticism places the writing of the book not earlier than the reign of Solomon, which was from 1015-975 B. C., nor later than the return of Judah from Babylonish captivity, which occurred in 536 B. C. Orthodox writers, such as The Pulpit Commentary, Albert Barnes and others, place the date of the writing of the book before the Egyptian bondage or the giving of the law at Mt. Sinai. If their findings are correct, the book was written almost two thousand years before Christ. As evidence of the antiquity of the book it is argued that, if the book had been written since the Egyptian bondage or the giving of the law, some reference or at least some hint would be found in the book to that effect. It is further reasonably noted that, had the book been written since there was such a thing as Israelitish history, its very nature is such that the writer would have drawn upon that history to prove his conclusions. Throughout the entire book no such traces can be found.

Job and the Age in Which He Lived

According to the facts disclosed, we are dealing with a book which is very old, having been written well unto four thousand years ago. Further, Job may have lived some time earlier than the writing of the book, and his history handed down orally, from generation to generation, as ancient history was.

There are a few other things about the age in which Job lived, which point to an early date, that we should note:

As will be seen from the first chapter of the book, Job, as the father, was the priest—he offered sacrifices for his sons. This was patriarchal, and points to a date when there was not, as yet, an organized priesthood.

Then, too, no reference is made to a sanctuary, either tabernacle or temple, nor any stated place of worship. Evidently, then, Job lived in a day prior to the sanctuary or any organized priesthood.

Another thing is cited as an evidence of the fact that Job lived in a very early age. It is that the language used is what scholars call "archaic," meaning that the expressions found in the book are very ancient. All these evidences, taken together, are quite conclusive of the fact that Job lived in a very early time.

Job's Country

The name of the country in which Job lived was Uz. This name first appears in Bible history as the name of a man, the son of Nahor who was Abraham's brother (Genesis 22:21). The name again appears in Genesis 36:28. Later it became the name of a country, probably because of the descendants of one of these men occupying it. The land of Uz is located east of the sea of Galilee, or rather northeast of Palestine. It is now known as Hauran.

Its Historicity

The first question with which we are met, in discussing the Book of Job, is relative to its historicity, or its historical reality. This question must be intelligently approached and reasonably answered before satisfactory progress can be made in our meditations.

There are three views held concerning the historicity of the book which are as follows:
1. A fictitious writing or a drama.
2. Absolutely historical.
3. A historical setting with poetical expansion and embellishment.

These views will be separately considered with an effort to ascertain the merit or demerit of each.

1. To conscientious students of the Bible an interpretation of the Book of Job as a piece of fiction, or a drama, seems entirely unworthy and completely out of harmony with the spirit and dignity of the Bible. The very first verse of the book says: "There was a man." This does not sound like the language of fic-

tion, but is a plain declaration of a fact. Then the place in which he lived is designated and his name is given. This book, which is the inspired Word of God, would certainly not make such plain, straightforward, unmistakable statements like these to which there were no corresponding historical facts. Another thing which should make us hesitant to accept such interpretation, from the very first suggestion, is the fact that it comes from a source where considerable of liberty is taken with the Scriptures, known as higher criticism.

2. To conclude that the second-named position is correct, which insists upon a rigidly historical interpretation, may be over-reaching, from the fact that the larger part of the book is poetry, and poetry, from its very nature, requires some latitude for expression. Poets, today, are given some liberty for expression, even to the extent of changing accents and pronunciation of words, for the sake of rhyme and rhythm. It is not unreasonable that Hebrew poets would be allowed some latitude for expression, even when expressing in verse a historical narrative. Then, too, in the poetic parts figures of speech are employed by the speakers, which in their very nature permit of varied expression.

3. The third position, then, is the one which appears as correct. The book is historical. There lived a man whose name was Job, as well as others whose names are given. The entire background is historical, and whatever expansion or embellishment it contains is that which is perfectly in keeping with the narration of a matter of history in the form of poetry.

Another evidence of the fact that Job lived in history is that mention is made of him in subsequent Old Testament Scripture, as well as in the New Testament.

In Ezekiel the fourteenth chapter, the fourteenth and twentieth verses, Job is named together with Noah and Daniel. This testifies to the fact that he was considered a historical person, as truly as were Noah and Daniel, and no one seems to question the history of these men. James also, in the fifth chapter and eleventh verse, speaks of Job without any apology whatever.

When we keep in mind the fact that, though the hand of some man was used to pen the Book of Job just like any other book of the Bible, but that God inspired it, no difficulty is experienced. It is when we leave God out of the question that we encounter trouble. In this lies the trouble of the higher critic. Men, who consider the book from the standpoint of literature merely, have pronounced it "a very superior production." Studied in the light of inspiration, by the illumination of the Spirit and by the help which comes as a result of earnest prayer, the book appears as one of the most sublime ever written.

CHAPTER II
A PERFECT MAN

CHAPTER II

A PERFECT MAN
Job 1:1-5

THE unique character who becomes at once the central figure of the narrative is unceremoniously introduced to us as a "perfect" and "upright" man. Whatever may have been meant by this expression, it is evident that the qualities ascribed to Job were the very choicest and best attainable by men who lived in his day.

The term "perfect" means complete, entire, not lacking. The Greek word translated "perfect" is a strong one meaning *absolutely finished*. The first verse of the chapter continues to delineate his character, showing that his perfection had two sides. It had a positive side—he "feared God." It also had a negative side—he "turned away" from evil. In the statement that he "feared God" is included his whole attitude of reverence, worship and service. It was not "fear" in the sense of being afraid, but in the sense of obedience and trust. His turning away from evil bespeaks his attitude toward everything that was unworthy, sinful, or that would displease God. Unlike much of the religion of today, which has only one side, Job's religion had two sides—not only a positive which resolves, and attempts to do things, but also a negative side, which caused him actually to turn his back upon the "evil." To him there were some things which he could not do; some things which were unquestionably wrong, from which he turned away.

Persistency of His Perfection

Whatever that something was which Job possessed, which rendered him worthy of being called a "perfect man," it remained with him with surprising persistency.

Twice did God testify in heaven, in the presence of angels, to Satan, that Job was a "perfect" and "upright" man (1:8; 2:3). It was also understood by his wife, for while he was in the very midst of his second trial, with all its inexpressible bitterness, she asked him: "Dost thou still retain thine integrity?" (2:9). The word "integrity" is used in our English versions, but the Hebrew word is the same one translated "perfect" in the first verse, and would read accordingly: "Dost thou still retain thy perfection?"

Despite the insinuations which were cast upon Job, which would likely have more or less of a tendency to intimidate almost any person in his religious profession, Job professed perfection, right in the face of his accusers (9:21). Then with a tenacity which resembled a death grip, he declared he would hold it fast, saying: "Till I die I will not put away mine integrity [perfection] from me. My righteousness I hold fast and will not let it go" (27:5, 6).

Various Standards of Perfection

Having noted God's testimony to Job's perfection, as well as his own persistent profession of it, a little further inquiry into the study of the subject of perfection is necessary for a clear understanding.

Perfection in the absolute sense of the word, or absolute perfection, belongs to God alone, and can not be applied to man; consequently it is to the realm of relative perfections where we will be obliged to turn to find a perfection applicable to Job.

In the realm of relative perfections will be found all standards of perfections which are less than absolute. Here is *angelic perfection,* but since angels are of a distinctively higher order than man, this perfection is not suited to Job. Here also is *creation* or *Adamic perfection,* but since, by the fall, man has been reduced to a lower plane both physically and intellectually, as well as morally, this perfection is not suited to one in Job's situation. Here is also *resurrection perfection,* but that obtains only beyond the grave, hence sheds no light upon the subject of Job's perfection.

In the catalogue of relative perfections there remains yet a single one. It is that of *religious* or *Christian perfection* and is the one which Job possessed. This relative perfection which we speak of as religious or Christian perfection is a sliding scale. This scale is not adjusted to accommodate our notions, ideas or practices, but according to the revelation God has made of Himself. As that revelation has been progressive, the standard of religious perfection, with which God measures men, has been gradually rising, until today, as a result of the greatest revelation God ever made of Himself to the world, which was Jesus Christ, the standard is at the highest point it has ever reached.

In Job's day this relative perfection could not have been called Christian perfection, as it may now be called, but religious perfection, only. As the revelation can not lessen, the standard can not lower. God does not even measure men by the light which they have, but by the light He has made it possible for them to have by His revelation. The standard, then, with which God measured men in Job's day was a lower standard than that with which He measures men today. Should any one be tempted to offer any criticism of Job's words or conduct, he should remember this fact.

Lest some one fail to understand the subject of perfection, let it be noted that Christian perfection does not place men beyond the possibility of falling, although it greatly reduces the probability; does not make infallible, nor render immune from mistakes or errors in judgment. It deals with the heart more particularly than the head. It means that God's work of grace provided in the atonement of Christ is completed, finished or perfected in that individual.

His Piety

The standard of religious life experienced by Job was productive of great piety, as is evidenced by his devotions (1:5).

His devotions were family-wide: He made sacrifices for all his children. On the altar of his devotion, offerings were made for every member of his family, regardless of expense or any other consideration, though they numbered seven sons and three daughters (1:2). In Job's day man could not approach God without bringing with him the blood of his offerings, but such offerings were made to the number of them all. Family devotion was expensive in his day. The perfect offering having now been made, which was Jesus Christ, we may bring as a free gift, upon the altar of our devotions, the merits of His atoning blood. Yet professedly religious fathers, unlike Job, neglect the family-wide, pious devotion.

Further we note that these offerings were made "in the morning," preceding the labors of the day. No more opportune time could be found for such devotion than the morning. At this time God's gracious care during the unconscious hours is thankfully recounted, and His guidance for the waking hours earnestly sought.

One thing more which impresses us concerning this devotion is its unbroken regularity, expressed by the word "continually." No pressing labor nor busy season could deter Job from his devotion. No presence of friend or stranger could intimidate him. To him this was a matter of vital concern, and he could not afford to pass the opportunity by, for a single time. Religion was the important thing in his life, compared to which ordinary affairs appeared of little consequence.

His Family

Though not necessarily related to the subject of Job's Perfection, we must not pass unnoticed his interesting and ideal family which consisted of seven sons and three daughters. Although the children numbered ten, not one was overlooked nor forgotten in the unbroken family devotion.

His Riches

The possessions of Job were unusually large, consisting of seven thousand sheep, three thousand camels, five hundred yoke of oxen, and five hundred she asses. For the grazing of the sheep, camels and asses, and the cultivation for five hundred yoke of oxen, a large amount of land would be necessary. Allowing ten acres for each team of oxen, five thousand acres would be required for cultivation alone, besides the pasture land. He also had "a very great household," meaning man servants and maid servants. All these things point to the fact that Job was a great man, probably one of the greatest men of his day. He was God's man, whom He had chosen as a world example, and, as will be seen later, Job is placed on exhibition to men, devils and angels as an example of righteousness, to be thoroughly tested.

CHAPTER III

THE FIRST CHALLENGE

CHAPTER III

THE FIRST CHALLENGE
Job 1: 6-12

THE author of the book gives to us a very unusual opportunity. Holding aside the curtain which prevents our view of the eternal world, he gives us a glimpse of the council chamber of heaven, and permits us to hear a part of the conversation which took place at that particular convening of the heavenly council.

The meeting was one at which the "sons of God" came together, meaning, no doubt, the angels. There are evidently times when the angelic host comes together, into the very presence of God, to render to Him homage, to report their doings, and to receive His mandates.

Strange as it may seem to us, at first, there appeared at this heavenly council a personality very unlike the sons of God. His name is said to have been Satan. Shocked at the presence of Satan in this heavenly council, we hasten to make inquiry who he is, what his occupation, and what his mission is here. Zechariah saw him standing at the right hand of Joshua, the high priest, to be his adversary (Zech. 3: 1, 2), and St. John discovers him to be the accuser of the brethren, who accuses them before God day and night (Rev. 12: 10).

When asked by God from whence he came, he replied: "From going to and fro in the earth." Satan's own answer indicates his field of activity, "the earth." This no doubt means the earth in contrast to heaven where he has been cast out. His field of operation, then, is the human heart, the human family, and all that belongs to the lower plane. This testimony harmonizes with what Jesus confessed Satan to be, "the prince of this world" (John 14:30). Paul also speaks of him as the "prince of the power of the air, the spirit that now worketh in the sons of disobedience" (Eph. 2:2).

Satan also acknowledges his untiring and unceasing activity in his reply: "Walking to and fro." St. Peter speaks thus of him: "Be sober, be watchful: your adversary the devil, as a roaring lion, walketh about, seeking whom he may devour" (1 Peter 5:8). Here also his unceasing vigilance and activity are testified to.

While there are those who would interpret this "Satan" as not being identical with the Satan of the New Testament, but rather a servant of God, all evidence goes to prove that he is the adversary, the accuser, the slanderer, the devil mentioned throughout the Bible. He appears first in the garden of Eden, and last when cast into the bottomless pit (Rev. 20:10). His record from Genesis to Revelation has been the same, and no good word can be said concerning him.

A question which is perfectly legitimate is almost sure to arise at this time. It is, how came Satan to be present at the heavenly council? There is a satisfactory answer to this question, and the same will be given a little later, where he is seen to appear again at the second convening of the heavenly council. There is one assurance, however, which is, that his operations will some time cease for ever, as we have seen from the above-cited text, which reads: "And the devil that deceived them was cast into the lake of fire and brimstone, where are also the beast and false prophet; and they shall be tormented day and night for ever and ever."

God's Challenge to Satan
(Verse 8)

Turning our attention again to the heavenly council, we hear God challenging Satan concerning Job, saying: "Hast thou considered my servant Job? for there is none like him in the earth, a perfect and upright man, one that feareth God, and turneth away from evil." The Pulpit Commentary paraphrases this text as follows: "Thou that art always spying out some defect or other in a righteous man, hast thou noted my servant Job and discovered any fault in him?" It is certainly a great thing for God to speak thus of a man, realizing that He judges not from outward appearances, but from the heart.

Satan's Reply
(Verses 9, 10 and 11)

Immediately Satan replies to God's challenge, charging that Job serves him from selfish motives, and that a "hedge" has been set around him, shielding him from the temptations and trials which others are obliged to meet and endure. "Doth Job fear God for naught? Hast thou not made a hedge about him, and about his house, and about all that he hath on every side? Thou hast blest the works of his hands, and his substance is increased in the land." Here Satan may have reviewed the riches of Job, which have been previously enumerated.

It is easy enough to be good, reasons Satan, when a man is rich, and possesses all his heart can wish, especially when shielded from temptation and trial by a special providence. "Put forth thy hand now, and take away all that he hath, and he will curse thee to thy face." Replying to Satan's accusation of having made of Job a favorite, extending to him special care, God says: "Behold, all that he hath is in thy power, only upon himself put not forth thy hand." Special note should be taken that, in the giving over of Job to be tested by Satan, God made certain restrictions. God knows the limit to which His saints can bear testing, and Satan has his boundary set by God, and can not go a step farther than God gives him permission. In this instance Job is given over for testing to the extent of Satan's accusations concerning him, and Satan is privileged to do anything he chooses with the things for which he declares Job is serving God.

Accepting the challenge, Satan goes from the presence of God. He may have believed that Job could be induced to curse God, knowing as he did the weaknesses of humanity, and having little confidence in man's sincerity in the worship of his God.

CHAPTER IV

THE FIRST TRIAL

CHAPTER IV

THE FIRST TRIAL
Job 1:13-22

THE scene now changes from the heavenly council to earthly activities. What Satan has been doing since going forth from the presence of God we are not told, but we now find Job's trial on, in the form of a calamity which is cumulative in its nature, one stroke following another in quick succession.

The First Stroke

The first stroke resulted in the loss of all his oxen and asses. The oxen were plowing, and the asses were grazing near them, and the Sabeans came and took them away. They also slew all of the servants, except one, who came, running to Job, and told him of the loss. The Sabeans were a people who lived, at an early date, in certain parts of Arabia. Sometimes the term was applied, in a general way, to the Arabs.

The Second Stroke

While the young man was telling Job of the carrying away of the oxen and asses, and of the slaying of the servants, another servant, the keeper of sheep, came and said: "The fire of God is fallen from heaven, and hath burned up the sheep and the servants, and consumed them; and I only am escaped alone to tell thee." This "fire" may possibly have been something like lightning, as certain other references to similar visitations of "fire" seem to indicate. See Numbers 11:1-3 and 2 Kings 1:10-14. This interpretation seems all the more reasonable when we take into account the fact that Satan is spoken of as the "prince of the power of the air," indicating that he, in some measure, controls the elements (Eph. 2:2). The destruction of the sheep and the servants, by fire from heaven, constituted the second stroke of the calamity.

The Third Stroke

Before the words were out of the mouth of the second messenger, another came and declared that the camels had been stolen. The Chaldeans had made out three bands and came upon the drivers suddenly, slaying all of the servants but one, and taking away the camels. The Chaldeans were probably early settlers in Babylonia. The making out of "three bands" indicates the tactics of Oriental brigands, for the purpose of being able to approach and to attack from three sides. The loss of Job's camel caravans, with their drivers, as well as whatever merchandise with which they may have been loaded, was a very heavy loss, and constituted the third and a very severe stroke in Job's first and cumulative calamity.

The Fourth Stroke

Severe as the former strokes have seemed, the fourth and last stroke was much more so. It was the instantaneous and accidental death of all his children, seven sons and three daughters. It was probably upon the birthday of the eldest son, as they were celebrating the same by a feast according to Oriental custom. Suddenly a strong wind blew upon the house and, tornado-like, caused the house to fall, killing the sons and daughters of Job, also the servants, excepting one, who bravely brought the sad message to the grief-stricken father.

Special Notes on Job's Calamity

The various strokes crowd each other hastily—"while he was yet speaking," is the language used to indicate the quick and rapid successsion. The world's history knows no parallel.

The calamity came in a day of great activity. "The oxen were plowing," and the camel caravans were doubtless upon journeys of commerce, etc.

Both the forces of nature and the cruelty of man combine to bring ruin upon Job. This shows Satan's control over both. It will be further noted that the forces of nature and cruelty of man alternate in their efforts to destroy him. This also testifies to the subserviency of both the forces of nature and wicked men to Satan.

Issue of the First Trial
(1: 20, 21)

Having noted the reply which Satan made to God when Job was named as a perfect man, and his acceptance of God's challenge, also the severity of the cumulative calamity which befell Job, we are made to wonder what may be the issue of the trial. Quite contrary to the expectation of Satan and his boastful remarks is the issue. Job "rent his mantle." This was an Oriental way of expressing grief. He "shaved his head," and by so doing put off even the adornment which nature gave him. He "fell upon the ground," thus assuming a reverential attitude, and remarkable, significant thing! "he worshiped." Many a man has seen his possessions go up in smoke, carried away by armies, or devastated by flood, but few at such times assumed the reverential attitude and "worshiped." Many have been called upon to give up a child, a parent, a father or mother, or some loved one, but standing beside the bier the attitude has frequently been that of heart rebellion, rather than heart worship. Job worshiped and said: "Naked came I out of my mother's womb, and naked shall I return thither: the Lord gave and the Lord hath taken away; blessed be the name of the Lord."

Verdict of the First Trial

(1:22)

Whatever any one else may say concerning Job, God's verdict of his first and sore trial was: "In all this Job sinned not, nor charged God foolishly." Although innocent of the fact that he had been given over to testing and was being made a world spectacle, Job proved himself a man of sterling character, possessed of a faith which could not be subdued by a most sudden and overwhelming adversity. Though he could not see Satan back of the successive strokes of his calamity, he seemed to see God back of all. Satan said Job would curse God, but he "worshiped." Keen must have been his disappointment when, instead of renouncing God bitterly, even unto curses, Job fell upon his face and worshiped!

CHAPTER V

THE SECOND CHALLENGE

CHAPTER V

THE SECOND CHALLENGE
Job 2:1-7

AGAIN the curtain is drawn aside and the heavenly council has again convened. Here, as upon the former occasion, the angels have come together, and Satan is again present. At the first council he may have been present as a spectator, a spy, or to criticise or accuse. Having found that one of the specific missions of Satan is to accuse, and that continuously, it is quite evident that this was his mission at the first heavenly council. This conclusion is also supported by the fact that God proposed a person to whom his criticisms or accusations might be directed, resulting in the challenge, the acceptance of that challenge, and the calamity of Job.

At this meeting Satan is present with a stated purpose—"to present himself before the Lord." No doubt chagrined and blushing with shame because of his defeat, he appeared before God, yet of necessity he must report the results of the challenge concerning Job. Though Satan has been defeated, he will not recant. He still feels that he will win out.

Special Note on Heaven's Court

At this point it is necessary to consider the question previously asked but not answered, "How came Satan into the council of heaven?"

The court of heaven is the court of the universe. Here, God, the Judge, sits upon His imperial throne, and it is here that men's cases are weighed in the balances. All the courts of earth are but vague unrealities compared to this court, where angels are the messengers and servants. Unseen by mortal eye, the cases of men are tried, in the presence of the Judge.

Satan's name, "adversary" or "accuser," makes him the prosecutor. Jesus Christ is declared to be our "Advocate" with the Father (1 John 2:1). An advocate suggests the idea of one who intercedes for or defends another. He was also promised by prophecy as a "Counsellor" (Isaiah 9:6). Here again the idea of an attorney is suggested. The picture is then complete—the throne occupied by the Judge of the Universe, with Satan appearing on the one hand as the prosecutor, and Jesus Christ appearing on the other hand as the defense. It is in this court of heaven where accuser or plaintiff (Satan) and Advocate or Defense (Jesus Christ) meet face to face and argue the cases of men in the presence of the Judge.

Again the question is asked, "Why does God allow Satan such liberties as these?" Perhaps the best answer to this question is, that this is God's way of retaining a righteous superiority over Satan. It is necessarily in keeping with God's dignity, justice, superiority and glory that Satan, who is His rival, and who was thrust out of heaven because of his ambition, as an archangel, to be equal with God, should be given opportunity to present his claims. Even Satan must and does receive justice at the hands of God. That this is God's way of retaining a righteous superiority is indicated by the fact that at the close of the millennium, during which time Satan will have been bound, he is to be loosed for a little season, to try God's work (Rev. 20:7, 8). It should be yet noted that Satan is only allowed to appear in the court of heaven as a subdued foe, and dares not venture to speak or to present his case except upon God's invitation.

God's Second Challenge
(2:2, 3)

Satan having appeared at the second convening of the heavenly council, God again addresses him, asking him from whence he came. As if hesitant about discussing the subject of the former challenge and defeat, he replies: "From going to and fro in the earth, and from walking up and down in it." Breaking the silence upon the subject, the Lord said to him: "Hast thou considered my servant Job? for there is none like him in all the earth, a perfect and an upright man, one that feareth God and turneth away from evil: and he still holdeth fast his integrity, although thou movedst me against him, to destroy him without cause." It will be noted that God speaks about Job, in this second challenge, in the same terms as He did in the first, even adding extra emphasis upon the character of Job. Although he has undergone a calamity, unparalleled in the world's history, God has not changed His mind concerning him.

Satan's Second Reply
(2:4, 5)

With an answer which seems to be premeditated, Satan replies to God by saying: "Skin for skin, yea, all that a man hath will he give for his life. But put forth thy hand now, and touch his bone and flesh, and he *will* curse thee to thy face." Property and family have little significance compared to one's life, reasons Satan. If Job's body is afflicted, "he *will* curse thee to thy face." To this the Lord replies, "Behold, he is in thy hand; only spare his life," and Job is given over for further testing. It will be noted that again restrictions are placed on Satan, and beyond these limitations he can not go. He was privileged to subject Job to anything by way of disease and suffering, but dared not take his life. God never gives a saint over for testing without placing the restriction. He knows how much His servant can bear, and Satan can not go beyond it.

Still, determined to accomplish the undertaking in which he had failed—to cause Job to curse or renounce God—Satan accepts the second challenge, goes out from the presence of God, and plans a calamity calculated to reach the farthest limits of the restriction placed by God.

CHAPTER VI

THE SECOND TRIAL

CHAPTER VI

THE SECOND TRIAL
Job 2:7-10

THE scene is again changed. Satan having accepted God's second challenge begins his operations. Could Job only have known what we now know, it might have helped him to bear up under the pressure of the trial, but such knowledge would have spoiled God's plan of giving to the world an example of righteousness thoroughly tested.

The First Stroke
(2:7, 8)

The first stroke of Job's second calamity came in the form of extreme affliction. Having searched the catalogue for the most trying, most painful, most disgusting disease, Satan selects this one of which Job becomes the subject, and he is smitten with sore boils from the crown of his head to the soles of his feet. The disease is thought to have been elephantiasis, so named because the swollen limbs and blackened, rough skin appear like the skin of an elephant.

Symptoms of Job's Disease

The following are a few of the symptoms of Job's disease as cited by Prof. Davidson.

It was accompanied by intolerable itching. "He

took him a potsherd to scrape himself'' (2:8). So terrible and deep-seated was the itching that the nails of his swollen fingers could not relieve the distress, so he took broken pieces of pottery (potsherd) with which to scrape himself. It is almost impossible to imagine such a condition of bodily suffering as this.

It disfigured his countenance. His friends "knew him not" (2:12).

It caused his breath to become fetid, and the odor drove persons from his presence (19:17).

His sores bred worms (7:5).

His disease caused his body to be swollen and emaciated, alternately (16:8).

He suffered unearthly dreams (7:14), and restless nights (7:4).

It caused his bones to burn (30:30) and his limbs to feel like one with his feet in the stocks (13:27).

As a result of this intense suffering and inexpressible anguish he was frequently caused to long for death. Death to him would indeed be welcome.

The Second Stroke
(2:8)

This disease with all of the suffering resulting from it would seem almost more than mortal man could endure. He who experiences such affliction should be provided with the best of comforts and have the tenderest hands to administer to him. Instead of this, as a second stroke in Job's second trial, he was segregated. "He sat down among the ashes." This evidently means that Job was segregated outside of the walls of the city, and was compelled to find lodgment among the refuse or garbage. He did not have so much as a pest-house or an isolation hospital to receive him. We look upon the convenience of pest-houses and isolation hospitals almost as a curse. To Job they would have been a comfort, but he was an outcast.

The Third Stroke
(2:9)

Adding to the first stroke of affliction and the second stroke of segregation, comes a third stroke which, if anything, is more severe. His wife becomes his spiritual enemy. "Curse God and die," is her advice to her husband, to whom life has no more charm, but who longed for relief. She allies herself with Satan and becomes his agent.

The German version of this text says: "Bless God and die," but that the English version is correct is evidenced by Job's reply. It is rather unfortunate that, in this instance, an original Hebrew word is used which under certain conditions is translated "bless" and under other conditions is translated "curse." The context alone must determine the translation and the meaning. This accounts for the two different translations of this verse.

That Job's wife has become an ally of Satan is evidenced by the fact that she advised Job to do exactly what Satan said he would do provided his body became afflicted. This proves Satan to be the author of her very words. Here Satan again shows his diplomacy. Well does he remember how in the Garden of Eden he had employed a woman to tempt the first man, and how successful were the results. Again he shrewdly employs a woman as his agent, to tempt Job, and expects to be successful as in the former case. Further, Job had been rendered most susceptible to temptation by sickness and his former calamity. We must not forget that Job was innocent of the fact that God was making of him a world example of righteousness tested, or the case would be entirely different.

This third stroke of Job's second and cumulative calamity is all the more severe when we think of whom the person was who became his enemy and Satan's ally. It was his wife—she whom he had loved as a maiden, to whom he had vowed and who had vowed to him lifetime faithfulness. It was she who was the mother of his ten children, who are all now dead; who had shared with him his joys and sorrows. What an exceedingly sad thing to have his wife, the bride of his youth, the mother of his children, now dead, to assume such an attitude! Prof. Pierson says: "Mrs. Job spoke but once, but it would have been to her credit had she kept still."

Issue of the Second Trial
(2:10)

Remembering the challenges made by God concerning Job, to Satan, in the heavenly councils, also the former defeat of Satan in trying to cause Job to curse his God, and thus prove that righteousness is merely a pretense, that those who serve God do so from selfish motives only, we can not but be vitally interested in the issue of a trial of this nature. Robbed of all his property; childless because of apparent providential calamity; afflicted beyond description; his wife, the one above all others who should help and comfort him, now appears before him and subtly betrays him. As surely as Satan was back of the kiss which betrayed our Lord, it was he who prompted and directed this betrayal. Shall Job fall? Shall he curse his God? The issue of the trial depends upon the attitude which he assumes. Should he do as Satan declared he would, God's case would be lost and Satan's won.

With a keen sense of spiritual perception, Job detects the folly of his wife; and though he does not understand it, he accepts his calamity as coming from God. Perhaps Job spoke better than he knew when he said: "Shall we receive good at the hand of God, and not evil?" While the evil which was coming to him was not **from** the hand of God, but that of Satan, it was permitted **by** God, who stood ready as He always does in behalf of His children, to transform His curse into a blessing. His faith reached farther than the curse, and even now began to claim deliverance. Having discovered the folly of Mrs. Job, and having exercised faith in his God when he could not see nor understand, he severely rebukes his wife by saying: "Thou speakest as one of the foolish women speaketh." Conscious of her own guilt, the stinging and straightforward rebuke of Job proves sufficient, and Mrs. Job is not heard from again throughout the entire book.

Verdict of the Second Trial
(2:10)

Whatever may be our opinion of the outcome of Job's second trial, we are anxious to know God's verdict. He has kept watch every moment, has heard every word and knows even the secret thoughts of Job's heart. Without preamble or apology, here is God's verdict: "In all this did not Job sin with his lips."

As truly as the trials were cumulative, so were the verdicts. The verdict of the first trial was: "In all this Job sinned not, nor charged God foolishly." The verdict of the second trial is: "In all this did not Job sin with his lips." Not even in word was Job guilty of having sinned. Here is a man's most subtle temptation—to murmur or complain, if not to curse—and we are reminded of a New Testament quotation: "If any stumbleth not in word, the same is a perfect man, able to bridle the whole body also" (James 3:2). It was perfection which God had claimed for Job, and the second trial now being over, the cause of perfection is vindicated and the docket is clear. The judge has spoken the verdict, "acquitted." Whatever may result in the future trial of Job, the world has now an example of righteousness tested and triumphed. Expressing the verdict in the most charitable manner, Satan has failed in his second attempt to overthrow Job, and, unless he can devise some more successful plan, is destined to final defeat.

CHAPTER VII

THE THIRD TRIAL

CHAPTER VII

THE THIRD TRIAL
Chapter 2:11—37:24

FOR what reasons we do not know, but we are introduced to Job's third trial, without having been permitted to hear the conversation which took place between God and Satan at the close of the second trial. Should some one argue that there was no "third trial," he should note that the second trial has ended; that we have already seen the "issue" and have heard the "verdict." That there was a third trial is evidenced by the fact that, at the close, there is another verdict of a cumulatively strong nature. This fact will be made clearer later on, but is mentioned here because some interpreters deny a third trial.

Having heard of the affliction of Job, three men came to visit him. They were:

>Eliphaz the Temanite.
>Bildad the Shuhite.
>Zophar the Naamathite.

These men came from various countries and from localities quite a distance apart. Eliphaz came from Tema, a place in the eastern part of Idumea. Bildad was a descendant of Abraham through Keturah and Shuah, but his home is unknown. Zophar probably came from a place in Arabia.

It is also evident that they met together by appointment and came. What significance the phrase "by appointment" may have, may be an interesting and a disputed question; but it is quite probable that a careful study will disclose the fact that he who "appointed" the elements and the wrath of men to bring calamity upon Job in his first great trial, and who "appointed" horrible disease and betrayal from his own wife as a second and greater calamity, also had some relation to the "appointment" of these three men whose visit and whose speeches with all that they contained constituted the third, and greatest of his trials. May this not be the third, stubborn, prolonged and final effort on the part of Satan to destroy Job's faith, upon which Satan's success or defeat depends?

Further, they professed to be friends, and probably had been. The customary Oriental expressions of sympathy and grief were observed:

> They wept.
> They rent their mantles.
> They sprinkled dust upon their heads.

Orientals are very emotional and express grief by wailing. They also rend their garments, symbolically reflecting their grief, which, as they think, rends their hearts. As a further act of humiliation they put dust upon their heads, making a very unsightly appearance. These expressions of grief were practiced by Job's friends, continuing for seven days, during which time they sat down with Job upon the ground, not speaking a word to him. Though they may have spoken together, not a word was spoken to Job in this period of time. Some one has said that their grief was so great that they could not speak, but there is probably a better answer to the question of their silence. The days of their weeping were seven. This was the exact period of time devoted to weeping for the dead, as will be found by reading Gen. 50:10. It is evident, then, that upon reaching Job they found his condition such that they treated him as though he were dead and as though they were in the presence of a corpse. He was so changed in his appearance that they knew him not, and perhaps the only thing which they thought remained to do was to bewail him and return to their homes. The silence was broken by Job, when he began to speak, and as a result an interesting conversation follows:

Job's Lamentation and Its Meaning
(Chapter 3)

The silence of the seven days of mourning was broken by him who was being bemoaned as dead. Prompted by all of the cumulative calamities which had befallen him and by his inexpressible sufferings, and probably by the strange actions and suspicious conduct of his visitors, he speaks, not to them, but in their presence.

We have now arrived at a point in the discussion of the Book of Job where it is necessary to detain with a brief, critical study, since much depends upon a correct understanding of Job's conduct under the successive and cumulative strokes of the first and second trials. If Job did what Satan said he would, the case is lost, and God is defeated. Let us see.

There are six words in the Hebrew language in which the Old Testament was written, which may be translated "curse." There are only three of these which need enter into our investigation.

Arar is the strongest word, and never means less than to curse. In the active voice it means to pronounce an anathema upon some person or thing. In the passive voice it means to have a curse pronounced upon one. It is the word which is used where God told Abraham that He, Himself, would curse the one who would dare to curse Abraham (Gen. 12:3). Though this word does appear once in the Book of Job, it is not used to predicate anything concerning Job's conduct.

Qalal is another Hebrew word translated curse, and is also found in the verse cited above. Of the three Hebrew words which we shall consider, *qalal* is the mildest. The promise to Abraham reads: "And I will bless them that bless thee, and him that curseth thee will I curse." In this single statement two Hebrew words translated curse are used. There is significance to this. Let us substitute the Hebrew words for the English, and the line reads: "Him that *qalals* thee will I *arar*."

The word *qalal* sometimes means to curse; sometimes to revile, and sometimes to speak lightly of a person or thing. As is the case with many Hebrew words, the context alone must determine their translation. The line then translated literally may well be: "Him that speaks lightly of thee will I curse."

Barak is the third Hebrew word, translated sometimes curse or renounce, and sometimes bless. It is the word used in Job 2:9, where of Job's wife it is said that she told Job to "renounce God, and die." In this instance, Luther's German version translates the line, "bless God, and die." It is evident from the context that the German version is incorrect, but the context alone must determine the translation, since in some connections the word means to bless, and, in others, to curse. *Barak* is the second strongest of the Hebrew words coming within the range of this study. This brief perspective upon Hebrew words which may be translated curse orients the reader into the problem of the interpretation of Job, at this point.

Now to the critical question: How interpret Job's conduct?

For emphasis, let it be repeated, that the strongest Hebrew word, *arar,* is not used at all in connection with Job's accusation or conduct.

Returning to chapter 1, verse 11, Satan told God that if He would touch Job's property, he would renounce (or curse) Him to His face. Here the word *barak* is used, which might mean either to bless or to curse. It can not mean the former; therefore must mean the latter. In chapter 2, verse 5, Satan is reported to have said to God: "Put forth thy hand now, and touch his bone and his flesh, and he will renounce thee to thy face." The word *barak* is again used, and must mean curse, or something uncomplimentary. The word "renounce" is employed by the translators. Here are the two accusations made against Job by Satan, and the meaning of his accusations is evident. The King James Version uses the word "curse" to translate the Hebrew word *barak* in both of these challenges of Satan to God.

There is another shade of meaning conveyed by the Hebrew word *barak,* as is given in Young's Critical Concordance. It is that of turning away from, or bidding farewell to. According to this meaning of the word, Satan declared to God that under certain unfavorable conditions which he named, Job would bid farewell to God and cease to serve Him. This meaning is in harmony with Satan's insinuation when he said: "Doth Job fear God for nought?" (1:9). In the light of this probable meaning of the Hebrew word used in his accusations against Job, the whole book must be read and carefully studied to determine whether Job did what Satan said he would.

But since so much apparently hinges upon Job's lamentation as found in the third chapter, it is necessary to give to it careful and critical consideration.

It is certainly unfortunate that the American revisers employed the word "curse" in the first verse of the chapter, making the line to read: "Job opened his mouth and cursed his day." In this translation the American Version follows the King James Version. Accordingly the unskilled and superficially thinking reader throws up his hands and concludes that Job has done exactly what Satan said he would, and God's case is lost. If this were true, the only world example which God ever held up to men, angels and devils as a specimen of righteousness, would have proved a disappointing failure; Satan would have been honored; God would have been defeated—an occasion for weeping on the part of men and angels. This is, however, a wrong translation, a wrong interpretation, and an erroneous conclusion, as we shall see.

The word translated "cursed" in Job 3:1 is not *arar*, the strong Hebrew word for curse. Neither is it the next stronger word, *barak*, which is used in Satan's challenges to God concerning Job (2:5), sometimes translated "bless" and sometimes "curse,"

JOB A WORLD EXAMPLE

dependent upon the context, but doubtless here meaning to renounce, in the sense of turning away from. But the milder word, *qalal*, which means to revile, or to lightly esteem, is used. The reader can easily see that there must have been a divine purpose in the choice of this word in recounting Job's reaction to his severe and testing trials. The translation would then be more likely correct, if it should be made to read as follows: "Job opened his mouth and reviled [or spoke lightly of] his day," meaning the day of his birth.

Then, too, it is strange that the object of cursing, or reviling, or lightly esteeming, whichever it be, on Job's part, has been overlooked. It was not God, but the day of his birth which came in for treatment. Had he pronounced a curse or an anathema, it would not have been upon God, thus doing what Satan said he would, but upon the day of his birth. Whatever fault may be lodged against Job for esteeming lightly, or reviling, the day when he was born, there is a world of difference between this and cursing or turning away from God.

Tracing Job's lamentation in chapter 3, we discover that there is progress in it. First, he regrets that he was conceived, and born. Then, he wishes that it might have been his good fortune to have died at birth. Since he was conceived and born, and did not die at birth, he can not understand why his life must be prolonged in this miserable state. This is a summary of Job's lament.

While there may be little to gain by comparing one Old Testament character with another, there is nothing to lose by so doing. Jeremiah lived in a much later time than Job, and had advantages far superior to his. Furthermore, Jeremiah is listed among the greatest of prophets. By examining the twentieth chapter of Jeremiah's prophecy, beginning at verse fourteen, it will be found that he did exactly the same thing which Job did. The only difference between the two laments is in Job's favor, for in recording the words of Jeremiah, the strong Hebrew word for curse, *arar,* is used. The line reads: *"Cursed* be the day wherein I was born. * * * *Cursed* be the man who brought tidings to my father * * * ."

Closing the discussion on Job's Lament, a line from Butler's Bible Work, Volume on Job, is pertinent: "The dispute between God and Satan concerning Job was not whether Job had infirmities (which must have been granted) but whether he was a hypocrite, and secretly hated God, and under provocation would prove it."

CHAPTER VIII

LIBERAL AND CONSERVATIVE VIEWS

CHAPTER VIII

LIBERAL AND CONSERVATIVE VIEWS

BEFORE pursuing our study further, taking up the speeches of Eliphaz, Bildad and Zophar, which bitterly arraign Job, constituting successive strokes in his third, lingering and cumulative calamity, it will be found interesting and profitable to note the liberal and conservative views concerning Job's "Comforters" and Job himself.

Concerning Job's Comforters

Liberal View

1. Present-day, liberal interpreters see in these men deep piety and pure motives.
2. They look upon their conclusions as being based upon the early Hebrew conception of God as in direct relation to the world, doing all that is done, without recognizing the intervention of second causes. Consequently, if evil comes upon a man, God sends it; and back of that evil there must be sin in the life, which is being justly punished.
3. That the speeches of these men are, in the main, consistent, and are purely the result of a desire to befriend Job, and to help him into right relation with God.

Conservative View

1. Conservative interpreters find, in the speeches of these men, ignorance, assumption and even dishonesty.

2. Whether or not these men are conscious of their alliance with Satan, they are looked upon as tools of his, and as being directed by him in a final and lingering effort to cause Job to do what he had prophesied that he would do—curse God.

Concerning Job

Liberal View

1. Job has been overcome with the difficulties with which he has met and needs rebuke. He is self-righteous and must be chastised.
2. He has, in his complaint, well nigh approached a cursing of God.

Conservative View

1. Job's speeches, although proceeding from anguish indescribable and physically unendurable, have in them a deep tone of assurance and submissiveness.

2. Although he challenges the Almighty to manifest Himself and solve the problem of his life, it is with the consciousness that he is innocent and perfect before Him, and expects to be exonerated.

3. Job has not sinned. There is no occasion for speeches such as were made by these three men, and there is no explanation other than that they are of Satanic design.

Things to be Considered in Connection with the Study of Job's Words and Conduct

1. The emotional nature of Orientals.
2. The unenlightened age in which he lived—many centuries before Christ came.
3. The extreme severity, multiplicity and cumulativeness of his calamities.
4. The provocation he received from the suspicious looks and bitter words of his "friends."
5. He had no written promises of grace, divine presence, help and deliverance, such as we have today. A single written promise such as "God is faithful, who will not suffer you to be tempted above that ye are able; but will with the temptation also make a way of escape; that ye may be able to bear it" (1 Cor. 10:13), or, "We know that to them that love God all things work together for good" (Rom. 8:28), would have given him an anchorage and certainty such as he did not possess. Job's critics should place themselves in his day and circumstances before speaking harshly of him.
6. Living before Israelitish history, there were no historical incidents of similar character which could possibly shed any light upon his case.
7. He was human and likely to err as well as we, but had access to the Advocate to plead his cause for error unwittingly or innocently committed, as well as we.
8. The "perfection" which Job possessed was not absolute but relative, God only having absolute

perfection. Neither was his angelic perfection, for that belongs only to angels. Adamic or creation perfection was not his, for that belonged only to man unmarred by sin. It was not resurrection perfection which he enjoyed, for that places men beyond mortality, which Job is suffering inexpressibly. It was religious perfection, or the completion of the work of Grace in his heart and life, which met every requirement of heaven, enabling God to look upon him as a "perfect man"—one who stands complete or finished so far as the work of Grace is concerned.

9. The scale of relative perfection, which God adjusts in keeping with the revelation He makes of Himself, being lower in Job's day than in ours, the standard with which He measured Job was not the standard with which He measures men today.

10. Though Job possibly said things, at times, which are inconsistent with our light and knowledge, they were not with his. Critics of Job overlook this. It was the case of a wrong head and right heart. In his accusers it was a case of wrong heads and wrong hearts. This is evident from the final verdict and Job's Divine Vindication.

Advance Conclusion

Job did nothing and said nothing which was contrary to the standard of "perfection" which God required of men in Job's day

CHAPTER IX

THE FIRST CYCLE OF SPEECHES

CHAPTER IX

THE FIRST CYCLE OF SPEECHES
THE THIRD TRIAL—Continued
Chapters 4-14

FOLLOWING the lamentation of Job, begin three cycles of speeches. Each one, Eliphaz, Bildad and Zophar, speaks three times, excepting that Zophar drops out in the third cycle. In each case they are answered by Job.

We will note each speech made, and Job's answer, and in every case we shall try to find the keynote. In some instances only a few verses will be quoted, which will indicate the character of the speech. Should any one think our selections partial, in any way, correction will be thankfully received.

First Speech of Eliphaz
(Chapters 4 and 5)

The first speech of Eliphaz, which is the first speech made, will be examined quite carefully, as it establishes a precedent which was imitated by the other speakers, and may be said to be the keynote of all that follow:

> "If one assay to commune with thee, wilt thou be grieved?
> But who can withhold himself from speaking?
> Behold, thou hast instructed many,
> And thou hast strengthened the weak hands.

> **Thy words have upholden him that was falling,**
> **And thou hast made firm the feeble knees.**
> **But now it is come unto thee, and thou faintest;**
> **It toucheth thee and thou art troubled.**
> **Is not thy fear of God thy confidence,**
> **And the integrity of thy ways thy hope?**
> **Remember, I pray thee, whoever perished, being innocent?**
> **Or where were the upright cut off?**
> **According as I have seen, they that plow iniquity,**
> **And sow trouble, reap the same.**
> **By the breath of God they perish,**
> **And by the blast of His anger are they consumed."**
>
> 4: 2-9.

The very first part of the first speech of Eliphaz is a thrust at Job. He charges him of having been able to comfort others under affliction, but now, when he himself is afflicted, he is fainting. Neither does it stop with this thrust at Job's courage, and patience, but the speaker indicts Job's innocency and uprightness:

> **"Whoever perished being innocent?**
> **Or where were the upright cut off?"**

He proceeds to an argument based upon a well-known law of nature:

> **"They that plow iniquity,**
> **And sow trouble, reap the same."**

The conclusion is that Job is reaping iniquity and trouble, consequently he must have sown the same.

Eliphaz then proceeds by relating a spirit vision which he had:

> **"Now a thing was secretly brought to me,**
> **And mine ear received a whisper thereof,**
> **In thoughts from the visions of the night,**
> **When deep sleep falleth on men,**
> **Fear came upon me, and trembling,**
> **Which made all my bones to shake.**

> Then a spirit passed before my face;
> The hair of my flesh stood up.
> It stood still, but I could not discern the appearance thereof;
> A form was before mine eyes:
> There was silence, and I heard a voice, saying,
> Shall mortal man be more just than God?
> Shall a man be more pure than his Maker?
> Behold, He putteth no trust in His servants;
> And His angels He chargeth with folly:
> How much more them that dwell in houses of clay,
> Whose foundation is in the dust,
> Who are crushed before the moth!
> Betwixt morning and evening they are destroyed:
> They perish forever without any regarding it.
> Is not their tent-cord plucked up within them?
> They die, and that without wisdom." 4: 12-21.

The relating of a spirit vision attracts special attention, and often produces unusual effect. Waiving, for the moment, the question of the truth or falsehood of the vision, it manifests diplomacy upon the part of the speaker.

Let us now investigate the spirit vision which caused the speaker's hair to stand up, and which he possibly recited in hushed tones, for sake of effect. The principal thing which interests us is the message which the spirit is reported as having spoken:

> "Shall mortal man be more just than God?
> Shall a man be more pure than his Maker?
> Behold, He putteth no trust in His servants;
> And His angels He chargeth with folly:
> How much more them that dwell in houses of clay,
> Whose foundation is in the dust."

Listening to the message which the spirit is reported to have brought, we can not but note the strangeness of that message, and how unlike what we have heard in the heavenly council. God has not charged His angels with folly, neither His servants. Instead, He challenges Satan, himself, to test His servant, Job, whom He twice declared to be "perfect" and "upright." O Job, if we could but tell thee what we have seen and heard, the story of the spirit vision would not disturb thee! But this we dare not do, or God's plan of making thee a world example would be spoiled.

Spirit visions need always to be carefully considered. "Try the spirits" was as good advice in Job's time as today. Beware of the man who has seen a spirit vision in the night. The object of the speaker was, evidently, to undermine Job's faith in God and deny his relation to God. Whether or not the speaker was ignorant of the deceptions of spiritism, as many are today, really believing in communications in this manner, and being made the tool of Satan, may be a difficult question; but it is evident that Satan, through the speaker, was making a diplomatic effort to impress Job, the suffering listener, with the things absolutely contrary to God's nature and what He has said. God said, "Job, my servant, is a perfect and upright man." The spirit said: "He putteth no trust in His servants." Yea, more, "He chargeth [even] His angels with folly." The "accuser" is still at work. As truly as Mrs. Job became the mouthpiece of Satan, so also Eliphaz.

Turning again to the spirit message, we detect in it a personal thrust of Satan at God. Satan who was one time a shining archangel was cast out of heaven because he sought equality with God. This, of course, occurred during the period of angelic probation in the heavenly world, which has long ago ceased as man's probation will some time. As a fallen archangel he is God's enemy, determined to overthrow God's work. In this spirit message he puts into the lips of Eliphaz a thrust against the justice of God, attempting to justify himself, to indict God, and to destroy Job's faith in God.

Among other things which Eliphaz said was:

> "Behold, happy is the man whom God correcteth.
> Therefore despise not thou the chastening of the
>   Almighty." 5: 17.

Job should receive these chastenings as a correction from God, and count himself happy, so reasoned Eliphaz.

Job's First Reply to Eliphaz
(Chapters 6 and 7)

Replying to the first speech of Eliphaz, Job replies that his calamity is beyond measure:

> "Oh, that my vexation were but weighed,
> And all my calamity laid in the balances!
> For now it would be heavier than the sand of the
>   seas:
> Therefore have my words been rash." 6: 2, 3.

Continuing, he expresses his intense suffering:
> "When I lie down, I say,
> When shall I arise, and the night be gone?
> And I am full of tossings to and fro unto the
>   dawning of the day.
> My flesh is clothed with worms and clods of dust;
> My skin closeth up, and breaketh out afresh."
>   7: 4, 5.

Friends show kindness to one in distress, even if, as Eliphaz has said concerning Job, he has forsaken God; but Job has been deceitfully dealt with. The pity he should have is denied him.

> "To him that is ready to faint kindness should be
>   showed from his friend;
> Even to him that forsaketh the fear of the
>   Almighty.
> My brethren have dealt deceitfully as a brook,
> As the channel of brooks that pass away;
> Which are black by reason of the ice,
> And wherein the snow hideth itself."   6: 14-16.

Bildad's First Speech
(Chapter 8)

The second speaker, Bildad, now addresses Job. His speech is not so lengthy, and does not advance anything particularly over what the former speaker has said, except to suggest that Job is probably being punished for the sins of his children:

> "If thy children have sinned against Him,
> And He hath delivered them into the hand of their
>   transgression;
> If thou wouldest seek diligently unto God,
> And make thy supplication to the Almighty;
> If thou wert pure and upright:
> Surely now He would wake for thee,
> And make the habitation of thy righteousness
>   prosperous."   8: 4-6.

Note again Satan has put into the mouth of the speaker a denial of the very thing which God affirmed, the uprightness of Job. He also takes advantage of the death of Job's children and makes a painful charge of their sins. Although Job has been pious, and daily brought his sons and daughters to God by his sacrifices, and though Satan has, himself, brought about their death, it is all charged against Job. The accuser again has found human lips through which to speak.

Toward the close of Bildad's speech he seems to be-

JOB A WORLD EXAMPLE 83

come sympathetic, and if we may hope that he is not speaking sarcastically, gives Job a few words of consolation:

> "Behold, God will not cast away a perfect man,
> Neither will He uphold the evil doers.
> He will yet fill thy mouth with laughter,
> And thy lips with shouting.
> They that hate thee shall be clothed with shame;
> And the tent of the wicked shall be no more."
> 8: 20-22.

Job's First Reply to Bildad
(Chapters 9 and 10)

Bildad having finished, Job proceeds to answer him, reviewing God's omnipotence in a way which has surprised the greatest astronomers and students of nature. His reference to "Arcturus" (the Great Bear), "Orion" (the Giant), "the Pleiades," and "the Chambers of the South," now well-defined arrangements of constellations, prove that the science of astronomy was well developed in the ancient days when the Book of Job was written. Perhaps better, the mention of these things, so far in advance of the development of the science of astronomy, proves the inspiration of the book. God, of course, knew the heavens far better then than we do now, and could put into the mouths of His speakers things which they did not understand. Taking into account the astronomy in the Book of Job, that found in the writings of the Psalmist, as in Psalm 19:1: "The heavens declare the glory of God," etc., no wonder that the great astronomer and naturalist, Sir Isaac Newton, should have said that he could get more astronomy by reading his Bible a single hour, than by watching in his observatory all night.

Job's rehearsal of God's omnipotence is given in the following sublime sentences:

> "Of a truth I know that it is so:
> But how can man be just with God?
> If he be pleased to contend with Him,
> He can not answer Him one of a thousand.
> He is wise in heart, and mighty in strength:
> Who hath hardened himself against Him, and prospered?
> Him that removeth the mountains, and they know it not,
> When He overturneth them in His anger;
> That shaketh the earth out of its place,
> And the pillars thereof tremble;
> That commandeth the sun, and it riseth not,
> And sealeth up the stars;
> That alone stretcheth out the heavens,
> And treadeth upon the waves of the sea;
> That maketh the Bear, Orion, and the Pleiades,
> And the chambers of the south;
> That doeth great things past finding out,
> Yea, marvelous things without number." 9: 2-10.

After the review of God's omnipotence, Job proceeds to review his case. Although he can not understand, he insists upon his guiltlessness and says:

> "Thou knowest that I am not wicked,
> And there is none that can deliver out of Thy hand." 10: 7.

Zophar's First Speech
(Chapter 11)

At the close of Job's reply to Bildad, Zophar, the last of the trinity of speakers, addresses him. From the very first word he unsparingly scathes Job, accusing him of a "multitude of words," even "boastings" and "iniquity," proceeding thus:

> "Should not the multitude of words be answered?
> And should a man full of talk be justified?
> Should thy boastings make men hold their
>   peace?
> And when thou mockest, shall no man make
>   thee ashamed?
> For thou sayest, My doctrine is pure,
> And I am clean in thine eyes.
> But O that God would speak,
> And open His lips against thee,
> And that He would show thee the secrets of
>   wisdom!
> For He is manifold in understanding.
> Know therefore that God exacteth of thee less
>   than thine iniquity deserveth." 11: 2-6.

Having finished his accusations against Job's words, and the uprightness of his character, Zophar advises Job to repent:

> "If thou set thy heart aright,
> And stretch out thy hands toward Him;
> If iniquity be in thy hand, put it far away,
> And let not unrighteousness dwell in thy tents."
> 11: 13, 14.

Job's First Reply to Zophar
(Chapters 12, 13, 14)

When professed friends came to visit Job he had reason to expect some words of comfort at least. They have all three now spoken, and instead of consolation he has received accusation. In their efforts to prove their superior wisdom, they have drawn conclusions which Job recognizes as absolutely false. Job now proceeds to answer Zophar, addressing them all by the use of justifiable and appropriate irony:

> "No doubt but ye are the people,
> And wisdom shall die with you." 12: 2.

Continuing, Job claims understanding also:

> "But I have understanding as well as you;
> I am not inferior to you:
> Yea, who knoweth not such things as
>   these?"
> "What ye know, the same do I know also:
> I am not inferior unto you."   12: 3; 13: 2.

It is not the contention of Job's professed friends that God has sent upon him his calamity, to which Job objects, but their conclusions as to the cause for which his calamity has been sent. Job even assumes that both animate and inanimate creation have such wisdom as that, and replies:

> "But ask now the beasts, and they shall teach thee;
> And the birds of the heavens, and they shall tell
>   thee:
> Or speak to the earth, and it shall teach thee;
> And the fishes of the sea shall declare unto thee.
> Who knoweth not in all these,
> That the hand of Jehovah hath wrought this,
> In whose hand is the soul of every living thing,
> And the breath of all mankind."   12: 7-10.

Relative to their conclusions as to causes, and the remedy they suggest, Job replies:

> "But ye are forgers of lies;
> Ye are all physicians of no value.
> Your memorable sayings are proverbs of ashes,
> Your defences are defences of clay."   13: 4, 12.

Probably due to the fact that all of the three visitors have spoken to his keen disappointment, bringing him no comfort, Job, having reviewed their shallow wisdom and false conclusions as above, again declares that though he should be slain, yet he will trust in God (13: 15).

Then, after reviewing his own mysterious and hopeless condition, he compares himself to

> "A rotten thing that consumeth,
> Like a garment that is moth-eaten."   13: 28.

Immediately Job takes up a pathetic strain and utters words which have been read beside many biers and open graves since his day:

> "Man that is born of a woman,
> Is of few days, and full of trouble.
> He cometh forth like a flower, and is cut down:
> He fleeth also as a shadow, and continueth not.
> And dost thou open thine eyes upon such a one,
> And bringest me into judgment with thee?"
>   14: 1-3.

Seeing that all mortal hopes have failed, Job catches a gleam of future immortality, and raises the question, reasoning from nature as follows:

> "For there is hope of a tree,
> If it be cut down, that it will sprout again,
> And that the tender branch thereof will not cease.
> Though the root thereof wax old in the earth,
> And the stock thereof die in the ground;
> Yet through the scent of water it will bud,
> And put forth boughs like a plant.
> But man dieth, and is laid low:
> Yea, man giveth up the ghost, and where is he?
> As the waters fail from the sea,
> And the river wasteth and drieth up;
> So man lieth down and riseth not:
> Till the heavens be no more, they shall not awake,
> Nor be roused out of their sleep.
> O that thou wouldest hide me in Sheol,
> That thou wouldest keep me secret, until thy wrath be past,
> That thou wouldest appoint me a set time, and remember me!
> If a man die, shall he live again?

All the days of my warfare would I wait,
Till my release should come.
Thou wouldest call, and I would answer thee:
Thou wouldest have a desire to the work of thy
 hands." 14: 7-15.

CHAPTER X

THE SECOND CYCLE OF SPEECHES

CHAPTER X

THE SECOND CYCLE OF SPEECHES

THE THIRD TRIAL—Continued
Chapters 15-21 Inclusive

Second Speech of Eliphaz
(Chapter 15)

THE second cycle of speeches is introduced by the second address of Eliphaz, who, having listened to the first addresses of Bildad and Zophar and Job's replies, arrives at the conclusion that he has a most certain indictment for Job. Accusing Job of craftiness and iniquity, he declares that Job's own words convict him:

> "Should a wise man make answer with vain knowledge,
> And fill himself with the east wind?
> Should he reason with unprofitable talk,
> Or with speeches wherewith he can do no good?
> Yea, thou doest away with fear,
> And hinderest devotion before God.
> For thine iniquity teacheth thy mouth,
> And thou choosest the tongue of the crafty.
> Thine own mouth condemneth thee, and not I;
> Yea, thine own lips testify against thee."
>
> 15: 2-6.

Evidently feeling that Job has not, as yet, been sufficiently impressed with the spirit vision related in his former address, Eliphaz again refers to the message which he claims was brought to him, and says:

> "What is man, that he should be clean?
> And he that is born of a woman, that he should
>   be righteous?
> Behold, he putteth no trust in his holy ones;
> Yea, the heavens are not clean in his sight:
> How much less one that is abominable and corrupt,
> A man that drinketh iniquity like water!"
>
> 15: 14-16.

Job's Second Reply to Eliphaz
(Chapters 16 and 17)

At the close of the second address of Eliphaz, Job replies, characterizing the visitors as "miserable comforters." Further, he assures them that if they were in his place, and he in theirs, he would speak words, not of accusation and contempt, but words of comfort and solace:

> "Then Job answered and said,
> I have heard many such things:
> Miserable comforters are ye all.
> Shall vain words have an end?
> Or what provoketh thee that thou answerest?
> I also could speak as ye do;
> If your soul were in my soul's stead,
> I could join words together against you,
> And shake my head at you.
> But I would strengthen you with my mouth,
> And the solace of my lips would assuage your
>   grief." 16: 1-5.

Job finds no possible way of accounting for his fearful and indescribable misery, except that it is God-permitted, but continues to plead his own innocence, and appeals to God in heaven as his witness:

> "Although there is no violence in my hands,
> And my prayer is pure.
> O earth, cover not thou my blood,

And let my cry have no resting-place.
Even now, behold, my witness is in heaven,
And he that voucheth for me is on high.
My friends scoff at me:
But mine eye poureth out tears unto God,
That He would maintain the right of a man with
   God,
And of a son of man with his neighbor!
For when a few years are come,
I shall go the way whence I shall not return."
16: 17-22.

Second Speech of Bildad
(Chapter 18)

In his second address, Bildad seems to have forgotten the kindly feeling which we had thought he entertained for Job in the closing of his first address, and becomes bold in his accusations, the entire address being a tirade against Job, comparing him to the wicked who will be driven from the face of the earth, leaving no posterity, remembrance or name in all the earth:

"How long will ye hunt for words?
  Consider, and afterwards we will speak,
Wherefore are we counted as beasts,
And are become unclean in your sight?
Thou that tearest thyself in thine anger,
Shall the earth be forsaken for thee?
Or shall the rock be removed out of its place?
Yea, the light of the wicked shall be put out,
And the spark of his fire shall not shine.
The light shall be dark in his tent,
And his lamp above him shall be put out.
The steps of his strength shall be straitened,
And his own counsel shall cast him down."

   *   *   *   *   *

"He shall be rooted out of his tent wherein he
   trusteth,
And he shall be brought to the king of terrors.
There shall dwell in his tent that which is none
   of his:

94 JOB A WORLD EXAMPLE

**Brimstone shall be scattered upon his habitation.
His roots shall be dried up beneath,
And above shall his branch be cut off.
His remembrance shall perish from the earth,
And he shall have no name in the street.
He shall be driven from light into darkness,
And chased out of the world.
He shall have neither son nor son's son among
  his people,
Nor any remaining where he sojourned.
They that come after shall be astonished at his
  day.
As they that went before were affrighted.
Surely such are the dwellings of the unrighteous,
And this is the place of him that knoweth not
  God." 18: 2-7 and 14-21.**

Job's Second Reply to Bildad
(Chapter 19)

Being sorely vexed by the second speech of Bildad, as well as all that had been said, Job replies:

"How long will ye vex my soul,
And break me in pieces with words?
These ten times have ye reproached me:
Ye are not ashamed that ye deal hardly with me.
And be it indeed that I have erred,
Mine error remaineth with myself.
If indeed ye will magnify yourselves against me,
And plead against me my reproach;
Know now that God hath subverted me in my
  cause,
And hath compassed me with His net." 19: 2-6.

Ignorant of the knowledge which we have been permitted to obtain, by the holding aside of the curtain, and knowing no other source from which calamities could come, Job looks upon God as the source. Pathetically he describes his condition, being entirely forsaken by his "brethren," his "acquaintance," his "kinsfolk," his "servants" and even his "wife":

JOB A WORLD EXAMPLE

> "He hath put my brethren far from me,
> And mine acquaintance are wholly estranged
>   from me.
> My kinsfolk have failed,
> And my familiar friends have forgotten me.
> They that dwell in my house, and my maids,
>   count me for a stranger:
> I am an alien in their sight.
> I call unto my servant, and he giveth me no answer,
> Though I entreat him with my mouth.
> My breath is strange to my wife,
> And my supplication to the children of mine
>   own mother.
> Even young children despise me;
> If I arise, they speak against me.
> All my familiar friends abhor me,
> And they whom I loved are turned against me."
>   19: 13-19.

Despite all this he declares his absolute faith in God:

> "Oh that my words were now written!
> Oh that they were inscribed in a book!
> That with an iron pen and lead
> They were graven in the rock for ever!
> But as for me I know that my Redeemer liveth,
> And at last he will stand up upon the earth:
> And after my skin, even this body, is destroyed,
> Then without my flesh shall I see God;
> Whom I, even I, shall see, on my side,
> And mine eyes shall behold, and not as a
>   stranger.
> My heart is consumed within me."   19: 23-27.

The statement, "I know that my Redeemer liveth," is a very significant one, and seems quite in advance of Job's day. In fact, this quotation is often confused with New Testament statements, being sometimes thoughtlessly credited to Paul. The surroundings and circumstances, so dark and unfavorable, make this testimony of Job's to sparkle with richer luster and beauty.

Second Speech of Zophar
(Chapter 20)

The second speech of Zophar, from beginning to end, will be found to be an arraignment of the wicked, which can not but be intended to apply to Job. Reference is made to a wicked man losing his wealth, of which Zophar evidently thinks Job is an example. Almost any verse indicates the attitude he assumes to Job, but the following are characteristic:

> "Knowest thou not this of old time,
> Since man was placed upon earth,
> That the triumphing of the wicked is short,
> And the joy of the godless but for a moment?
> Though his height mount up to the heavens,
> And his head reach unto the clouds;
> Yet he shall perish forever like his own dung:
> They that have seen him shall say, Where is he?
> He shall fly away as a dream, and shall not be found:
> Yea, he shall be chased away as a vision of the night.
> The eye which saw him shall see him no more;
> Neither shall his place any more behold him.
> His children shall seek the favor of the poor,
> And his hands shall give back his wealth.
> His bones are full of his youth,
> But it shall lie down with him in the dust."
>
> 20: 4-11.

Job's Second Reply to Zophar
(Chapter 21)

Job proves himself equal to the task. His professed friends have constantly, by direct and indirect statement and every conceivable figure of speech, accused Job of being a sinner, consequently being justly punished. Job reminds them that God permits even the wicked to be in health and prosper. The conclusion is that if God permits even the wicked to be in health and prosper, his own sufferings and adversity are not evidences that he has sinned. Accordingly he proves their conclusions and charges false, and closes his address by saying:

"How then comfort ye me in vain,
Seeing in your answers there remaineth only
falsehood?" 21: 34.

CHAPTER XI

THE THIRD CYCLE OF SPEECHES

CHAPTER XI

THE THIRD CYCLE OF SPEECHES

THE THIRD TRIAL—Continued
(Chapters 22-31 Inclusive)

Third Speech of Eliphaz
(Chapter 22)

THE third and final speech of Eliphaz is a vehement accusation of Job. He charges him with "great wickedness," even to the oppression of widows and orphans, and dishonesty in various forms. Having heard what God said about Job in the beginning of our study, we recognize these accusations of Eliphaz as downright lies, prompted by none less than Satan, who, from behind the curtain, is conducting Job's third and lingering trial. How any sane commentator or half-honest interpreter can sympathize with these hell-bred and Satan-designed accusations of Job is a mystery. Hear the fearful charges which fell from the lips of Eliphaz:

> "Is not thy wickedness great?
> Neither is there any end to thine iniquities.
> For thou hast taken pledges of thy brother for nought,
> And stripped the naked of their clothing.
> Thou hast not given water to the weary to drink,
> And thou hast withholden bread from the hungry.
> But as for the mighty man, he had the earth;
> And the honorable man, he dwelt in it.
> Thou hast sent widows away empty,

    And the arms of the fatherless have been broken.
    Therefore snares are round about thee,
    And sudden fear troubleth thee,
    Or darkness, so that thou canst not see,
    And abundance of waters cover thee." 22: 5-11.

Job's Third Reply to Eliphaz
(Chapters 23 and 24)

Despite all of Job's physical and mental suffering, he turns his heart and thoughts toward God, and declares his willingness to submit his case to Him, if only he might find Him:

> "Even today is my complaint rebellious:
> My stroke is heavier than my groaning.
> Oh that I knew where I might find Him!
> That I might come even to His seat!
> I would set my cause in order before Him,
> And fill my mouth with arguments.
> I would know the words which He would answer me,
> And understand what He would say unto me.
> Would He contend with me in the greatness of His power?
> Nay; but He would give heed unto me.
> There the upright might reason with Him;
> So should I be delivered for ever from my judge." 23: 2-7.

Job is certain of the outcome and still reposes absolute confidence in God, as is indicated by the following:

> "I have not gone back from the commandment of His lips;
> I have treasured up the words of His mouth more than my necessary food.
> My foot hath held fast to His steps;
> His way have I kept, and turned not aside.
> But He knoweth the way that I take;
> When He hath tried me, I shall come forth as gold." Chapter 23, verses 12, 11, and 10.

Bildad's Third Speech
(Chapter 25)

Having exhausted his resource, Bildad's third address is brief. Probably for the sake of emphasis he repeats the spirit-vision argument first produced by Eliphaz, that man can not be pure before God:

> "How then can man be just with God?
> Or how can he be clean that is born of a woman?
> Behold, even the moon hath no brightness,
> And the stars are not pure in His sight:
> How much less man, that is a worm!
> And the son of man, that is a worm!"   25: 4-6.

Job's Third Reply to Bildad
(Chapters 26-31)

Replying to the third speech of Bildad, Job persists in his own integrity:

> "As God liveth, who hath taken away my right,
> And the Almighty, who hath vexed my soul
> (For my life is yet whole in me,
> And the Spirit of God is in my nostrils);
> Surely my lips shall not speak unrighteousness,
> Neither shall my tongue utter deceit.
> Far be it from me that I should justify you:
> Till I die I will not put away mine integrity
>   from me.
> My righteousness I hold fast, and will not let it go:
> My heart shall not reproach me so long as I live."
>   27: 2-6.

The remainder of Job's reply is devoted to parables and the comparing of his present extreme contempt to his former greatness.

Third Speech of Zophar

Naturally we expect the three cycles of addresses to be unbroken, but the last speaker, Zophar, fails to appear in the third cycle. The reason of this is scarcely a matter of conjecture. The third speeches of Eliphaz and Bildad proved to be nothing but a repetition of former addresses, and the speech, especially of Bildad, very brief. Probabilities are that Zophar was entirely outwitted by Job, and he spared himself the humiliation and disgrace of not attempting to speak when he had nothing to say. In this one thing Zophar set an example still worthy of imitation. It was a silent confession of defeat.

Discourse of Elihu
(Chapters 32-37)

Though Zophar fails to speak in the last cycle, another proposes so to do. It is Elihu. Just when he appeared upon the scene we do not know, but judging from what he says, he has listened to most of the speeches made by Eliphaz, Bildad and Zophar, and Job's replies. He is a young man who is so full of words, desiring to show his "opinion" that he compares himself to a "wine-skin," ready to burst (32:19).

Having listened to the former speeches, his wrath is kindled against Job, because, as he interpreted it at least, Job was "righteous in his own eyes," and "justified himself rather than God." His wrath was also kindled against Eliphaz, Bildad and Zophar, because they found no answer, and yet condemned Job. Turning to the three speakers he chides them with the following words, professing to be perfect in knowledge:

"I am young, and ye are very old;
Wherefore I held back, and durst not show you
mine opinion.

JOB A WORLD EXAMPLE

> I said, Days should speak,
> And multitude of years should teach wisdom.
> But there is a spirit in man,
> And the breath of the Almighty giveth them
>   understanding,
> It is not the great that are wise,
> Nor the aged that understand justice.
> Therefore I said, Hearken to me;
> I also will show mine opinion.
> Behold, I waited for your words,
> I listened for your reasonings,
> Whilst ye searched out what to say.
> Yea, I attended unto you,
> And, behold, there was none that convinced Job,
> Or that answered his words, among you."
>   32: 6-12.

Proceeding, he addresses Job thus:

> "Howbeit, Job, I pray thee, hear my speech,
> And hearken to all my words.
> Behold now, I have opened my mouth;
> My tongue hath spoken in my mouth.
> My words shall utter the uprightness of my heart;
> And that which my lips know they shall speak
>   sincerely.
> The Spirit of God hath made me,
> And the breath of the Almighty giveth me life.
> If thou canst, answer thou me;
> Set thy words in order before me, stand forth."
>   33: 1-5.

Reviewing the spirit vision to which Eliphaz had twice referred and Bildad once, and accusing Job of presumption and self-righteousness he continues, professing to be the very mouthpiece of God:

> "Suffer me a little, and I will show thee;
> For I have yet somewhat to say on God's behalf.
> I will fetch my knowledge from afar,
> And will ascribe righteousness to my Maker.
> For truly my words are not false:
> One that is perfect in knowledge is with thee."
>   36: 2-4.

The speech of Elihu occupies six long chapters, to which Job listened, no doubt, attentively. When he was through Job answered him not a word. Prof. Pierson says that the reason Job did not answer Elihu was because he had not said anything. He had made much pretense and talked a lot, but said nothing. In vain may we search for any new thing Elihu advanced over what the others had said, although his wrath was kindled against them because they could not answer Job. His speech is almost entirely repetition. Here is another example of much talking with little saying— a good lesson, indeed, for such who are ready to burst with talk.

Classes which were taught by the author have been requested to check the words of Elihu against those of Eliphaz, Bildad and Zophar, with a view of discovering anything new which he might have advanced. One careful student reported that Elihu had struck one additional note, as found 34:37, where he accuses Job of rebellion. The lines read:

"**For he addeth rebellion unto his sin;**
He clappeth his hands among us,
And multiplieth his words against God."

Why Elihu drops out of the scene entirely it is impossible to say. That he is not later indicted by God, together with Eliphaz, Bildad and Zophar, has been interpreted by some as placing Elihu in a more favorable light. Since nothing more is predicated concerning him, the best thing is to dismiss him from our conclusions.

CHAPTER XII

DIVINE INTERVENTION

CHAPTER XII

DIVINE INTERVENTION
Chapters 38—42:6

THE scene is now entirely changed. God addresses Job from His pulpit, the whirlwind. Job has spoken words beyond his knowledge. There is not a hint in all that God said to Job, charging him with having sinned. Critics of Job are here challenged to produce any such charge. What God said concerning Job in the opening and closing chapters of the book would be unpardonably contradicted should we be able to justly interpret a single thing said in God's address to Job, as a direct or indirect charge that he has sinned. Grant that God did refer to Job when He said, "Who is this that darkeneth counsel by words without 'knowledge'," etc., the severest charge is of words without "knowledge," to which the saintliest man who lives today would doubtless be obliged to plead guilty, if God would address him in person. If lack of knowledge can be excused in this day, much more in the days of Job.

God's First Message
(Chapters 38:1—40:2)

God intends to give Job a vision of his own insignificance and, in order to do this, He gives him a review of animate and inanimate creation and propounds to him an exceedingly interesting but difficult list of examination questions, a part of which are as follows:

> "Where wast thou when I laid the foundations
>   of the earth?
> Declare, if thou hast understanding.
> Who determined the measures thereof, if thou
>   knowest?
> Or who stretched the line upon it?
> Whereupon were the foundations thereof fast-
>   ened?
> Or who laid the corner-stone thereof,
> When the morning stars sang together,
> And all the sons of God shouted for joy?
> Or who shut up the sea with doors,
> When it brake forth, as if it had issued out of the
>   womb;
> When I made clouds the garment thereof,
> And thick darkness a swaddling-band for it,
> And marked out for it my bound,
> And set bars and doors,
> And said, Hitherto shalt thou come, but no
>   further;
> And here shall thy proud waves be stayed?"
>   38: 4-11.

Also:

> "Who hath cleft a channel for the waterflood,
> Or a way for the lightning of the thunder;
> To cause it to rain on a land where no man is;
> Or the wilderness, wherein there is no man;
> To satisfy the waste and desolate ground,
> And to cause the tender grass to spring forth?
> Hath the rain a father?
> Or who hath begotten the drops of dew?
> Out of whose womb came the ice?
> And the hoary frost of heaven, who hath gen-
>   dered it?
> The waters hide themselves and become like stone,
> And the face of the deep is frozen.
> Canst thou bind the cluster of the Pleiades,
> Or loose the bands of Orion?

JOB A WORLD EXAMPLE

Canst thou lead forth the Mazzaroth in their
season?
Or canst thou guide the Bear with her train?
Knowest thou the ordinances of the heavens?
Canst thou establish the dominion thereof in
the earth?" 38: 25-33.

Job's Reply to God

Replying to these unanswerable questions propounded to him, Job answers:

"Behold, I am of small account; what shall I
answer Thee?
I lay my hand upon my mouth.
Once I have spoken, and I will not answer;
Yea, twice, but I proceed no further." 40: 4, 5.

God's Second Message
(Chapters 40: 6—41: 34)

Again God addresses Job out of the whirlwind, with a second list of questions. He now proposes that if Job can answer these questions satisfactorily, He will confess that Job can deliver himself (v. 14). In this list of questions special reference is made to the animal kingdom. God also invites Job to declare whether he is capable of ruling the universe. Of course, as no mortal man possesses these attributes and prerogatives of God, Job could not accept such a proposition as this. He can not deliver himself: he is gripped and held by the calamities which Satan has imposed in his effort to go every inch of the limitation God has marked out for him, in a final, unyielding purpose of causing Job to curse God. Satan will not set him at liberty; he can not extricate himself, and it remains for God to say it is enough, and the captive will be liberated.

Job's Second Reply to God

God's message to Job from His whirlwind pulpit constituted for him a new revelation. He had never known God thus before. What he had known of God previously compared to what he knows of Him now, is like hearsay compared to seeing, and Job exclaims:

> "I know that Thou canst do all things,
> And that no purpose of Thine can be restrained.
> Who is this that hideth counsel without knowledge?
> Therefore have I uttered that which I understood not,
> Things too wonderful for me, which I knew not.
> Hear, I beseech Thee, and I will speak;
> I will demand of Thee, and declare Thou unto me.
> I have heard of Thee by the hearing of the ear;
> But now mine eye seeth Thee." 42: 2-5.

It must be noted that Job determines to keep pace with the revelation which God has made to him of Himself, and proceeds to humble himself before the Almighty, declaring:

> "Wherefore I abhor myself, [margin, loathe my words]
> And repent in dust and ashes." Verse 6.

"Repentance" in this sense is natural for even innocent violations, as when one wrongs another unintentionally, as the result of error in judgment, accident, etc. An extreme incident of innocent violation is found in Deut. 19: 4-6, where a man accidentally killed another, and while he was innocent, had to flee to the city of refuge for safety. Job was not requested by God to "repent" and, whatever is meant by this statement, it is evident that what he did was voluntary upon his part.

JOB A WORLD EXAMPLE

Further, referring to the humbling of himself, humility is progressive. The great Apostle Paul said one time: "I am the least of the apostles" (1 Cor. 15:9). Later he said, "I am less than the least of all saints" (Eph. 3:8). Still later, speaking of great sinners, he said: "Of whom I am chief" (1 Tim. 1:15). Not now a sinner, but a chief sinner, saved by grace.

Likewise Job's increased light and revelation demanded a deeper humility, to which he freely and cheerfully responded.

CHAPTER XIII
JOB VINDICATED AND REWARDED

CHAPTER XIII

JOB VINDICATED AND REWARDED
Job 42:7-17

THE secret of the proper interpretation of the Book of Job will be found in its opening and closing chapters. The poetical portion of the book abounds in highly expressive figures, which can not be so certainly interpreted. It appears that so many lose themselves in the poetic part which is principally made up of the cycles of speeches, and fail to discover the one great and grand theme of the book which constitutes the title of this volume. In the complete vindication of Job which follows, it will be discovered that the book has a definite purpose, and that to have the Book of Job omitted from our Bibles would be a serious loss. Job is the only man, of which we have any record, whom God held up to the gaze of men, angels and devils, and made him "a world example." In this respect the book stands alone in its class.

Job's "Friends" Indicted
(Verses 7, 8)

Following Job's reply to God, which evidences that he had learned the lesson God intended to teach him—that of deeper humility—God addresses Himself to Eliphaz, Bildad and Zophar. These men, if they were permitted to be auditors when God addressed Job, were no doubt elated that, as they thought, God was humbling Job and thus exalting them. Keen must have been their disappointment when God addressed Eliphaz as follows:

"My wrath is kindled against thee, and against thy two friends; for ye have not spoken of me the thing that is right, as my servant Job hath. Now therefore, take unto you seven bullocks and seven rams, and go to my servant Job, and offer up yourselves a burnt offering; and my servant Job shall pray for you; for him will I accept, that I deal not with you after your folly; for ye have not spoken of me the thing that is right, as my servant Job hath."

A careful analysis of these verses discloses the following facts about Eliphaz, Bildad and Zophar:

1. *They have spoken wrong words.* Whatever they may have said which appeared as truth, in itself, was entirely discounted because the entire trend of their speeches was wrong, being inspired by evil purposes or motives, which God knew, and by which He judged them.
2. *God is angry with them.* "My wrath is kindled against thee and thy two friends." God being angry with these men proves the former conclusion, for God is not angry without a cause, and the things which these men had said were the things which kindled His wrath.
3. *They must repent.* There remains only one course for them to pursue. This command was enforced by a threat. Unless they repent, God will deal with them according to their "folly."
4. *Their sin is of such a nature as to require sacrifices.* "Take unto you seven bullocks and

seven rams." There is positively no other way; expiation was necessary: they have sinned and sacrifices are necessary.

5. *Further, they need some one who is worthy of the priestly office, to intercede for them.* No organized priesthood, in those days, to whom shall they turn? Strange as it may seem to us, and humiliating as it was to them, God selected the priest, naming Job. They may reject God's appointed intercessor, but if so God will reject them. "Him," says God, "will I accept."

Job's Vindication
(Verses 7, 8)

A careful analysis of these verses also evidences the following things concerning Job:

1. *He has spoken right things.* "Ye have not spoken of me the thing that is right, as my servant Job hath." Whatever he may have said which appears worthy of criticism, was entirely passed by or overlooked by God, because back of what he said was a motive which was fully justifiable.

2. *He is recognized still as God's servant.* "My servant Job." While God claims His "servant" Job, is there not an intimation that those who reproached Job are the "servants" of another? Whose servants, if not Satan's? Although accused and maligned, though charged with practically every sin but murder, by his three "friends," God still speaks of him as "my servant." Little difference does it make what

men may say of us or to us when God recognizes us as His servant.
3. *God required of him no repentance.* As noted previously, the attitude of repentance, which he cheerfully assumed when a new revelation of God came to him, was more particularly that of a sinking into deeper humility and reverence.
4. *He is promoted to the priesthood.* Job is permitted to officiate as priest at the altar where Eliphaz, Bildad and Zophar sacrificed their rams and bullocks, thus atoning for their sins, and receiving pardon.
5. *Job alone can intercede for them.* "Him will I accept, that I deal not with you after your folly." In a certain sense, Job held the destinies of these men in his hands. Apart from him and his prayers there is no forgiveness for them.

Strong Verdict

As Job's trials were cumulative, so the verdict of those trials. The first calamity came suddenly, stroke crowding stroke in such quick succession that the world's history knows no parallel. The verdict of that trial was: "In all this Job sinned not, nor charged God foolishly."

The second calamity which was severer, being a second and more strongly determined effort on the part of Satan to crush Job, heaps upon the first, and both weigh down upon him. The verdict of that trial which was so extremly bitter and unspeakably horrible was: "In all this did not Job sin [even] with his lips." As the lips are the instruments of complaint or any improper words, this verdict is exceedingly significant.

The third trial which was so tactfully planned, so stubbornly persistent and lingering, and which accumulated upon the first and second, now combines a trinity of calamities, either one of which has no peer in the annals of history. It is a third, hell-conceived, devil-plotted, thrice-determined effort of Satan to overthrow the only "perfect man" whom God has ever held up to be the target of hell, and to be gazed upon by men, demons and angels. Almost breathlessly have we stood awaiting the outcome. Should Satan succeed, a howl of hellish triumph will reverberate throughout the caverns of that dark place: angels would weep, and men fall low in the dust. Should Satan win, his superiority to God, his wicked ambition which cast him out of heaven, would have materialized, and across the heavens would be written in bold, blazing, taunting letters:

"**Mortal man can not be perfect before God.**"

But here is the verdict, not only spoken but acted: Satan's servants are severely indicted, and the only possible chance of reconciliation to God is by atonement. God's servant is completely vindicated, and becomes the only intercessor, before whom Satan's servants must fall, and by whom the forgiving ear of God can be reached in their behalf. Satan is defeated; "his assertions are so absolutely refuted and he is so completely discomfited that he passes into oblivion." —Pulpit Commentary. What a far-reaching and significant verdict! What a triumph for the possibilities of grace!

122   JOB A WORLD EXAMPLE

Job Rewarded

No trial reaches the saint without bringing its corresponding blessing. The stronger the trial, the greater the reward. Job's rewards were very great as are here enumerated:

1. When he prayed for his "friends" his own affliction was removed. Verse 10. Our ministry to others and our own blessings are so inseparably connected that we can not engage in the one without affecting the other.

2. His friends, who had forsaken him during the dark days of his calamity, came and renewed their friendship, at the price of gifts. Verse 11. "Truth crushed to the earth will rise again." Even men were compelled to recognize Job as worthy of renewed friendship and confidence.

3. God gave him double prosperity. Verse 12. Every item of his former possessions is doubled:
   Instead of seven thousand sheep, he now has fourteen thousand.
   Instead of three thousand camels, he now has six thousand.
   Instead of five hundred yoke of oxen, he now has a thousand yoke.
   Instead of five hundred asses, he now has a thousand.

4. Finally, Job is given the same number of sons and daughters—seven sons and three daughters—and his daughters were very fair. Being permitted to enjoy his increased possessions and renewed friendships, he was also privileged to look down upon four generations of posterity

JOB A WORLD EXAMPLE

even to great-great-grandchildren. "So Job died, being old and full of days."

Job's reward also constitutes another strong testimony to his innocence and complete vindication. God makes no mistakes. The Book of Job is no longer a "puzzle" but a beautiful, priceless revelation. Every life will be made richer and better because of this "world example." In conclusion, we are doubtless ready to extend the title of this little volume, making it read instead of: "Job a World Example," Job a World Example of Righteousness T-h-o-r-o-u-g-h-l-y Tested and F-i-n-a l-l-y TRIUMPHED AND REWARDED.